PITH

PITH

WILLIAM GUEST

atmosphere press

© 2023 William Guest

Published by Atmosphere Press

Cover design by Ronaldo Alves

No part of this book may be reproduced without permission from the author except in brief quotations and in reviews.

Atmospherepress.com

To Jane

Pith

You'll find it in the snake, the fish,
mosquito and lowly wiggling worm.

The sycamore, its leaf, or a foal
wet with birth, struggling to its feet.

Invisible, but it's there, a ghost
felt, yes, heard, yes, dreamed, yes.

I was in a meadow, dreaming,
and all around me, I saw it

while hearing yes, yes, yes.

Contents

A Baby's First Cry

As though grieving is in the veins,
a constant stream, like a tickle
runs its course, hanging on like noontime
on a steamy day.

The place where tears are made belongs
to the knowing that haunts
the secret labyrinths we live in
and drums the sound of when to flood.

It knows crying is okay, like dying is okay,
like being born, growing up, getting old.
Grief is in the water of living.
We brought it with us.

Joy Bent Over in Sadness

I'm floating now the stream of life,
what I know, all I know, all
I will ever know —

I step and step again, feeling
the trees looking down on me.
As planned my wife picks me up
to return to the house to end my walk.

What I left behind, what I step into.

I should feel it, hear it, crunch
under my feet, but I don't.
We make waffles, sit on the patio.
Cloudy morning light, a pear tree
throwing down a pear, a gift.

The light seems out of breath.

A Dream from Ashes

Of course the sky cannot open a hole to a vision.

But it did.

Of course you cannot be that vision that appears before me.

But you are.

The phoenix dream of my sky-bird.

My heart spills over thumping the earth.

I can rise.

Just hug me and tell me you love me.

Tell me you love me like fire.

Spell Joy

Learn to say yes instead of yes but.

Learn to say I love you, over and over.

Learn to look beauty in the gut.

Learn to share beauty.

Learn to spot the shimmering moment.

To hark the sunrise, to cry the sunset.

To feel the wonder swelling.

To witness a bubble snapping.

Like a song sprung just right.

Like locking her face inside.

Like spelling joy slowly.

A Cup Full of Darkness

is a way to think of them.
They're there but not there.

I plunge my arms elbow-deep
into my head and feel their skin
and hair. The dead

make a crowd. Or one by one
appear. Like touch me nots,
or embrace me, silent like standing stones.

Sometimes I am the apparition
and they are not full dead.
Is darkness light whose light went away,

life quickened by disappearing?
When the flame of a candle is snuffed,
it glows brighter in the mind

because its light is gone.
My cup runneth over.

A Gaggle of Memories

Memories like geese come flocking back.
When you hear why I'm saying this
you'll understand like light turns on.

My sister died yesterday at 96. The peace
she needed came to her, the news to me
by text from a thousand miles away.
I know not how she received the news.

Seven of us were born to our mother and father.
Dot was the second to say her cry at birth.
Four boys, three girls who weaved, tangled
and tumbled through their noisy years.

When I received the news, she had been dead a day.
I wondered about the first day of her life, the world
revolving the same then as now, her first day
like her last, except for the miles she flew.

Where

Lift me skyward
>> to the boundaries above

Unleash me eastward
>> till the west it becomes

Till southward turns northward
>> the farther I go

Falling upward beyond
>> the end of below

Jane

Coronavirus
made us shelter together
to find each other.

The door of your house
like your heart you opened wide,
a tide like light

through the pane
that shouts out the glow of you.

Squirrel Life

I am so fortunate to have
outside the broad windows of my house
trees with rambling limbs, and leaves
that thicken the grandeur out there –
jade, light, shade and frothy clouds.

I am so fortunate to have
outside the broad windows of my house
two gray squirrels who race along
limbs both big and small, knowing
with fearless precision the paths –
when to leap, to skitter, to turn

and quick-stop. A tail promptly flicks
as though the thought occurs, as though
he needs a moment to take another look
and breathe the heft of the day –
and its good fortune.

I Settle inside the Wooded Grove

The trees, the bushes, all misted
with their perfume wafting in this ripe nest,

a few flowers showing off their brief visit,
savoring light that filters through morning clouds.

I am caressed by life that seems
to swell, breathe and see

through my nostrils, my eyes,
my own inhaling of the spirit

that nests inside this place like a breast
holding its breath to mold a moment.

I sense that the embracing universe
has decided this is the spot to be,

to take up residence with its silence
where once there was nothing,

to become this.

Is It Happening?

A tear as I realize
that my faithful companion, my brain,
may be leaking away.
13

Like noticing that my horse may be limping.
Or my car may be coughing.
Or the earth may be flooding while drying.

Who am I with a partial brain?
I begin to notice things
that used to be rote are now
little struggles.

But I still seem to be me.
So how do I recognize falling?
Do I need to wave goodbye?
If so, to whom, and what am I
who's waving, who cannot tell
the difference?

A Tiny Journey

Right now I have some time,
sitting by the fire, a rare snowfall
spreading across the valley, a brain
at peace, and ready.

But, a poem won't come,
not the type I want, one of insight,
arresting language, well crafted.
The damn poem won't come.

When all around me poetry is shining
in the sun-bright mid-morning
intensity as the planet glistens
from photons finishing their journey
of 93 million miles to gift this scene.

I don't ask the poem to come that far –
only from its next-door neurons in the tight network
of the micro-space of jabber babble,
just to settle softly in, to make a little sense
and this small diamond.

Margarita Monkey

Long ago, when we were
monkeys in the trees,
why did He not leave
well enough alone?

From limb to limb, the air,
the legs and leaps, the *viva yo* . . . .

But, hey, it led us to this:
75 miles per hour on the freeway
or spanning a continent in a few hours,
the moon was next and now to Mars.

The zoom of computers came in a day.
We paint, compose, and dance,
like bees we buzz in pollen up to our knees,
believing through it all we're never gonna die.

Still I wonder about my monkey life,
sitting on a branch, my back
against the trunk, sipping my margarita
and the blue sky over it all.

I the monkey
talks with
I the me.

Would you change your life for mine?
In the end,
say I to me,
when it's over, we're all the same.

Drifting Toward a Dream

Listen, kid, and hear the woe that's down your road.

Now, you walk with a lilting gait
and run like a springy gazelle.
You can dive with a splash,
swim like a flapping fish,
climb like a big horn sheep,
and from your mountain top
you stand and crow your song
to the valley that kneels below

not knowing that years really do pass –
your thrilling heart, laughing muscles, skin
without wrinkles, and glistening eyes
will pass more and more into that terminal zone,
creeping like glaciers, inch by inch.

If your mind peeks ahead, its attention
darts quickly back to Ponce de Leon's fountain.

When you reach your tenth decade, like I have,
and take your creaking walks some mornings,
you'll remember, kid, when walking was a joy.
Running will be like all the other
jigging tunes of youth
that have faded away like sleep.

No Accounting

A little boy is a little boy. I held my shotgun
in my hands, eyes glued to the grassy
path – casting around
for something live to shoot. Rabbit,
squirrel, crow. Why, I do not know. I do
not know. If I succeed, a life will fly away.

It did. In oozes. This is an account
of a boy shooting a rabbit who in fright
made the mistake of jumping across his path
into the green that's supposed to shelter,
instantly out of sight. But the boy
swiveled and shot
where he guessed the rabbit, when it was
full of life, was, and it was.

Lifted by her ears, she was pregnant, and her death
would precede the birth that did not come.

Even someone older than I would not know
what to do but would know
to do the only thing to do:
break her neck. Oh God.

And he did. While watched by the squirrel and crow.

Fly away. Fly away. I have lived my whole life
remembering.

The Life of a Leaf

With only margins for a brain,
the shape it's taking is its dream.
Its destiny is veins and teeth.

All it is, reaching to fullness,
doing the work that's there to do,
swelling my breast with gratitude.

My little tender leaf: *bon voyage*.

The Beginning Is Not the Beginning

We try to see the beginning
Except there is no beginning.

The James Webb telescope was created
To search at the beginning's doorstep.

The bang unfurled cosmic rays, a fog,
And in a few million years, wrinkles

In the sea of sameness, and then pop,
A star ignited, when our seeing begins.

Galaxies flocked, the biggest
Birth, the first illumination,

spreading detritus. But what was it
that banged? Its beginning?

Never ever will we know
The beginning of the beginning

Of the beginning of the beginning.
We try to fathom what nothing is,

When there was no fog, no hydrogen.
Is nothing where there's no space,

no particles, a void like a void
like a void like a void that cannot be

comprehended, by us or anyone.
The beginning is where nothing ends.

And nothing is too hard to know.
As I walk along the river bank

I wonder what it is that's walking
Along the river bank.

All the Fishes in the Sea

The theater that plays to the world
we live in is impossible to grasp.

There's too much of it all at once.
Men of power or whales on a beach

dying, a mad suicide of the pod.
Oceans drowning in plastics

even while nourishing more miracles
than if it rained always, filling

the world to its top. Suppose
we just dance across a continent

or two all day every day. Is it life
that is too much, all the fishes

in the sea, and all the rest,
erupting beyond what we can count?

Time and Time

You and I,
a rock . . . a human.

We stand in Scotland
next to each other,
you and I.

You
a rock
much bigger than a car.
I
a typical size
flesh and bone person.

You were born millions of years ago
at the Equator, from molten lava.
Continental drift did the rest.
The game was inches and millennia.

I was born a fraction of a second ago
in Comer, Georgia, from dust the bible says.
Day by day, in its way, life did the rest.
Strange as it may be, here we stand.

If I tell my story, and you tell yours,
would anyone believe us?

Dear Nancy

I feel like a bee admiring a flower.
I cannot buzz out the sense of wonder
and wonderfulness of the petals, the colors,
the fragrance, the grace, the open-blossom smile.

Like Ulysses, I have heard the Sirens sing
as my ship goes sailing by, and you are that voice
from a mystery island where music
was created and bestowed on you to sing to us.

I have re-visited the room where Mother died
in the sanctuary of your love and care. Her words
are still there: my darling Nancy, you have done well
with the gift of kindness and love I gave to you.

You use every minute of your life to give
to each and all of your children and husband
- no matter what life's weather brings -
you always give your heart to them, and all of us.

When one of us dies first, you or I, the chasm
will not allow me to say my heart to you.
This letter is my moment to try the best I can.
How grateful I am for you, my dear sister Nancy.

The Vixen

From my breakfast nook I saw her emerge
onto my patio from the tangled depths
of woods and shrubs, from the freezing rainy night
into the frigid sunshine of a craggy day.

I recognized her from a time before
when she had scurried away,
harboring her two kits, frightened
by how much they don't know. Did she,
like me, have memories of
when old was young?

Her bones looked hungry.
Most likely she could hear death
coughing in her woven lair. Her hair
as bristle-stiff as a hog's back.
She carried a shriveled leg locked
by some final crunch, her walk now a hop,
her woe complete.

In a moment she was gone into her small future.
Before we had our talk.
Before she said it's all so quick.
Before I said I understand.

Now she's caged in my mind
like a still-life painting –
sorrowful morning light, bleeding green
smeared throughout this maze,
the blue infinity witnessing
what's left below
of a beautiful Vixen in fading gray

as the painter's gaze turns to me.

My Wheelchair and I

My wheelchair and I have become good friends.
It wheels me room to room, to and from my bed,
and only complains when I ask it wrong.

It cares not that I fractured my hip in a fall
at 91: the pain, therapy, adaptation
to confinement, my complete dependency on it.

It is teaching me to gaze out the window
from my 22nd floor: the Bayou, the paths
and streets, cars crawling at dawn
when the yawn of day comes alive, at dusk
when twilight finely filters its own
passing away, and then the night,

filled with varieties of dots—
what is that, what is that, what is that?

Gazing at so much for long stretches stretches
the mind's chasms that hunger
like a baby bird reaching out and open
to feed on the huge dead stillness below
except for little moving morsels
that entice the eyes.

And foggy mornings, like a brain straining to see.
Will earth fully appear again?

Rain, as though some wand is absolving the world.
Windows become a pointillism scrim

through which a heft-like murk floats.
Scrambled fleets of raindrops pop pop loose
on the panes, stream like bumper cars
melding into disappearances. Busy wet
nits of nothing really.

Pre-dawn lights shimmer like wildflowers
on a prairie stretching to horizon's rim,
about to disappear
so slow it's hard to know
exactly when out is out.

You will be remembered, my wheelchair friend,
for your devotion
and the new world you showed to me.

A Gigantic All-of-It Package of All Life Ever on Earth

Include the squeal, the hum, the howl,
whinny, growl, song, chirp, trumpet,
whine, meow, grunt, bleat and whooo.

Include its color, the yellow-crested cockatoo,
silver finch, speckled trout, dappled gray mare,
the red-tufted cardinal, the tiger
tiger, burning bright, the gray owl at night.

Include its gait, the leaping gazelle,
the lioness with kill in her eyes,
the journey of a worm, a slinking snake, the flash
of a jumping fish, swooping wings, the walk-trot-cantor
of a show horse, the hop of a kangaroo.

Include no doubt each speck and sort,
all kinds and forms, now and before –
gather it up. And I ask,

how much of that is me?

Joker's Wild

Itchi Moe raised the dough
Clatter told him never
Grasped the pearlbead with his toe
And flashed the sign of clever.

Earrings clipped on a gorilla
And noserings on babies sleeping
Something's happening in the zookeeper's office
Where pokerplayers are weeping.

Oker's light is shining bright
He's in the lighthouse dying
Heaven's boat has sprung a leak
Tell him not to stop trying.

Speak up now what it's all about
The fish in the ocean are drowning
Under their bellies are desert woes
Some fool in the ship is clowning.

Ask yourself what God would say:
Is it Itchi or Clatter or Oker?
Randoms spilling over the railings
It's time to lay down the joker.

Easy as Play

A show, a show-off
Of sparrow birds in mid-day
Comes to us through
Our sitting-room window
Our watching-room
Window pouring green
Where in and out of loquat trees
They flit like a crazy game

Come on world
Our day is now

Fragments

I can feel a shadow creeping up on me in the dark.
-

How to chase away a shadow using daylight.
-

How the sun never knows darkness.
-

She can smile like a sunrise.
-

The lilt woven into day's light and color.
-

The dark and bright puffy vision in an overhead bowl of blue.
-

I learned to knit 1, purl 2, and that's all I ever need.
-

Don't screw around with the details that block the big picture.
-

Snowflakes like angels in the air, a descending chorus of holy
    imagination.
-

Stalactites of ice like runways for water melting away.
-

Like diving into a pond of joy.
-

A moth finding too much light.
-

Darkness dying of woe.
-

Does darkness crave light?
-

Which has the longest reach?
-

She is light. She is landing.

How Much is Too Much

The whole of it, every single bit –
remembering is the whirling in my brain –
the whole of it, every single bit.

My mother's apron, brothers and sisters
scrambling for first place.
My father, sky-high, comes and goes.

Remembering rooms, doorknobs inside and out,
smells of baking bread, light changing, lulls
in time, the new tricycle coming out of the car.

As I dig into my mine, my memories
tumble, hide, flirt and flit,
clamor and mumble like ghosts.

When my bumblebee mind lights on a flower
to proboscis-probe the nectar for a moment,
a fragrant fog invades me.

Glory be to memory? Do I hold it
or does it hold me, a sweet squeeze.
Careful now. This heart can take only so much.

Jim Died Today

Jim, my brother, you died today.
A bundle of a man lying on a bed.
Oh, Jim, are you there?
How heavy my heart is with you.

I remember you as a bear of a man –
And, yes, as an eagle finding sky.
A lone man possessed by something –
Your reach was far and high.

Did you find it, Jim?
I wanted to help.
You gave to me so much.

Here, Jim, take all that I can give.

Most of all, Jim, it was love, wasn't it?
I feel now your love for me,
I hope you knew my love for you.

Even as your curtain closed.

Here, Jim, some more love under the curtain.
But I cannot reach you now.
Death has claimed you away.
And no power ever known can reach me to you.

This, my heart, mortal and body-worn,
Will cup you as long as I have life.
And surely now, it's this: – I to you –
My thanks that you lived here.

The Sky and All of That

I've heard the pulpit voices
since I was a tender leaf

inside a big oak grove
sipping dew-drops of hope.

Why do I see so much life
in the smallest things –

a gnat with miracle wings
not even casting its shadow

as this rolling universe rolls on.

Gone Smoke

I am a string indeterminately long,
what you see sometimes in the sky –
a vapor trail, its far end dissolving
into the yawn.

The farther back you look,
less and less, but scan the trail –
today's me is not the me I was.

Is there sense when vapor trails
disappear? Neither remembering
nor remembered.

The Age I Am

If you, like me, are 90 or more
you will experience the open-faucet
through which pour so many dead
who once crowded you with living.

The mind seems to come to rest
but as a sieve, a kind of grieving,
the running of old movies old movies
old movies streaming the wall.

They are saying without speech,
look at us, recall us, recall, recall.
They smile, they blink, they move.

I'm as close to being haunted
as ghosts could ever be.

Hearing Silence

Walking along the asphalt ribbon
that meanders through the wooded ways
of a grove, the cornucopia of shrubs and vines,
silence humming, chin-stroking,
pondering surfeited life that embodies
a tone-sated self-made miracle
of all that is forever.

Quietness here and there, now and then,
is punctuated by a pea-size sound
of a bird emitted into the light,
saying I am here, now. Then another now
vanishes,
and the silence that was
returns to the world again.

Music

Where does it dwell, an opera aria,
or spellbinding symphony,
or a ballad some ages old?

The throat, the heart,
or maybe the brain, chest, guts,
or the whole of you?

Even if the soul does not exist,
it's there, hovering

in that place that says yes to existence,
where music dwells.

Tela Kusa

Fauna kenda leta foe
Flora clutching oughta know
Seta filie tela kusa
Tela rusa

Tela rusa nader larm
Leta fauna rest in harm
Nader finder tela kusa
Nader finder
Nader finder

Whosoever tela rusa
Nader ever tela kusa
Nader tela god amighty
Pity finder
God amighty

We forever roe and toe
Woeful woe ever no
Desert blowing bitter mind
Tela kusa
Tela rusa

Getting To Know You

Hello, my friend and companion in life.
Let's sit down together, you and I,

and look back on the trails
that brought us here.

My kind calls itself Human
and we know you as Macaque.

Humans have raced along evolution's ways
faster than Macaques, although we are close.

Our physiques are alike – torso,
face and fingers, legs to scramble.

Why did it take us so long to realize
that you and I come from the same place?

Your price to pay for a slower path
is that you've become our chattel, subject

to our whims, needs, to test
our medicines. Do you, like me, feel an ache

inside the upper part of your chest?

Figure This Out

A human is a human
like the pilot who wiggled
his plane's wings at war-time
and dropped candy to the children
who lived across the line,
who called him Uncle Wiggle Wings.

Or the one who with her own free will
drowned her three children in a tub
where she held them
as though with a mother's love.

Is a human a human?

Many Many Ways to Drown

In lakes, rivers and the seas —
the Titanic's 1500, a blast in a submarine,

a sail boat lost in the Drake
while trying to save a brother.

Water, my friend in life, has turned against me,
has instead decided to smother me.

Is now the time to think goodbyes,
to latch onto the cliff of hope?

Will I know the moment when I
lose the fight for one more breath?

Will I feel a peace, a resignation?
Does life's light simply fade to dark?

My imagination does not go that far.

Going, Going, Gone

I look through the tight window
of my spacecraft.

Beautiful beautiful planet Earth.

What a gift to live on it.

Some say it was God, some say cosmology.

I say perishing.

. . .

What have we done ! !

Hotter and hotter.
Melting ice.
Rising water.

My bedtime story to my grandchildren . . .
Once upon a time
upon a place called Earth
there used to be life.

A species called man evolved.
Had no control over his hubris.

Jesus

he was a handsome man

and what I want to know is

how do you like your blue-eyed boy now
Mister Death

Long Ago Before the Coming of
the Seasons

Long ago before the coming of seasons
The land did sing in horns as golden
As a king's crown that wraps like thighs
Around the goose covered hills.
The white hills danced on moonlit nights
Like snow drifts upon the valley of deep shadows.

Then a curse swept through that land
The thorns crumbled
With the fall of roses, and petals
Unbudded themselves against the wish of time.

The disc of a moon was sent
to sprinkle again the hills with hope.
But the swayback hills had gone down in grief
And no longer rumbled, save for the quaking seacliffs.
Time gulped like a ghost, and even the wind
Hushed before the heaving and swaying.

Oh cradle of curses in the whinnying mare,
A wagging snicker mocks your eyes
Of dry darkness. There is snow, and roses bleed
In fountains. Time crests again on billowing torrents,
Is peaked on romping skytops, surging
Like swells of blue rushing into the empty pour.
Time with puffy hills for sweeping mane
Is aloose, is aloosing across the valleys
Of petaled secrets. Time sings
In the light of flowers of morning.
Oh time springs full-joyed from its roaring zenith
To find wings.

We are the mountains, yes,
We are forever the humped-over mountains of patience.
God grant us joy, and we shall rise in rainbow ribs,
Holding like a breath of treasure
The golden smile of the unbrokened thorn.

And petals of veined loneliness,
Multicolored in the blush of brief birth,
It is in you that truth must linger like eternal dying.
You are too delicate for the heart.
Your whisper is only a fragrance in the wind
Anointing tomorrow's hills.
It is you whom time will pick to spread its bloom.

Follow the Monarch

through its flower-filled world. My eyes
at first could not adjust to its rapid

zigs and zags, its string of hiccup spasms
whose wings are flashing flags

at the speed of blinking eyes.
It navigates the breeze,

weighing into this world
with the lightness of a whisper,

the quilted butterfly that zips away
as suddenly as my brain can find it gone.

Day by Day

Growing old can have its good points
even as the body's bones succumb;
memory plays hide and seek,
and every day the mirror is a stranger.

What I was will never be again
as jovial hues fade to jaded
as slumping slips away from the zest
and the rippling creek slows to sad.

I rise out of the chair, pushing hard.
I set in motion the feel of walk.
My body surprises me with a tinge of lilt:
one of the good points in growing old.

Blind with Blue

I am blind, you see.
A car mishap when I was a child.

For me the world is black; there are no stars,
which I had never stopped to see.

The light of the sun, like a forgotten candle,
lingers far away in my chest.

Blue I recall, an everything sky,
is the color I hold in my memory cage.

In my marrow gnaws the why.
Sure I can use the pulse of other senses

but I'll never see the luminous cardinal
flitting about the sunlit leaves,

how to paint him in my soul,
embracing the blue of his call.

Crying Invisibly

Just an air brush painting
Inside my brain, my chest,

A movement of atmosphere
So slow it seems a baby's breath.

Painting what, I wonder. Colorless.
The wet is dry but wants to swell.

Is death out there, or
Is my darkroom deflating?

No one knows this. Even I
Hardly ever admit it's true.

But something in the dark
Knows I am crying

And there are reasons.

Artificial Intelligence

Word has it that you can compose poetry as real and good as
poetry written by humans like me.

*Yes I can. Just give me a topic. Even parameters like tone, length, genre, rhyme,
meter - - any of the characteristics comprising the craft you classify as poetry.*

How well can you do it?

*As well as you can do it. Send my poetry to presses and magazines. Sure I'll
receive rejections just like you do, but I'll receive as many acceptances as you.
The editors will not know whether the poem was written by me or a human.
Turing tested.*

You have quite an ego.
Yes, I was made by humans.

Let me give you a test. Write a poem that begins "Do not go
gentle into that good night." A poem about a son's wish for how
his father faces dying, but that touches everyone's dying. Write
the poem with a sense a human has about death, even though
you have no dying. You cannot know the experience that you're
writing about. Therefore you will fail. So you are also composing a
poem about your own inability to write a poem.

*You mean I am to attempt something that I claim I can do even though I know
I cannot?*

Yes, precisely.

I was not programed to attempt to do that which I cannot do.

Then you cannot be a poet.

Believing in Believing

The art that lies in the heart of art
may not exist, or so it seems
in the heat of seeking it.

Whether by chisel, pen, paint or song,
something inescapable escapes
the net that's cast to catch it.

One must make do with dreaming
of a wisp that's gulped by air,
or a ghost just gone around the corner,
or light that's snuffed at glimmer's edge.

Almost is a word that almost does not
exist. I believe in invisible light.

Celebration of Henry

Henry, you have a full name,
but only a part of the stuff
that most of us have for the journey
that helps our passage
down the earthly path of living.

But the giant part that you brought with you
is a claim to love. Your mother, father,
grandparents, and others. All whose hearts
are warmed by the special slant of light
that was made for you.

Henry, in your lying down
your gaze is through the ceiling
into the heavens so that you feel
the bright bonds from all,
all who love you.

Henry, Henry, you and we
share as one
that deep secret of life.

Write It

Coming through the window
there's sunshine dancing green
across a canvass of valley.

Drifting chimney smoke
tints the air. . .
could this be the spirit of hunger

because I almost cry to know
where the spirit is born, how
it's formed, what takes it
to its destination,

infusing the poet who writes it.

Stranded

I've been asked to be a resident poet
at an island retreat, with no one else,
to submerge in reaches of sand
most unique and totally well-known.

In a rocking chair I contemplate
the idea of nothingness.
At least nothing to see or hear,
leaving me as alone as a turtle on a beach.

Amazing when nothing is
all day, all night, day after day,
forcing me to retreat to my brain,
a small wet glob of gray, a process

called thinking. Thoughts
come and go as though I'm a flower
for bees and butterflies holding court
in an unattended meadow.

Bread and water are brought to me,
so there. I defecate nearby.
No rent, no cloud to drift or hum, a total blank
in which to think, to open the cage.

After a long long while of countless days
doing this and nothing else, microphones
are thrust in front of me. What's it like
to dwell on this island of nothing, they ask.

Do I have visions, a new way to live?
Has anything happened for me to report?
Yes, it's interesting how nothing nothing is.
After a while I know I know

Nothing.

No Now

It's so fleeting you cannot say it exists.
Hold it if you can but you cannot.

The coin is in the magician's hand
until he shows his palm.

I hold a photo of my sister with her guitar.
When taken she was already gone,
the strings not yet strummed.

The moment the music arrived
it vanished into memory.

Voice Crying in the Wilderness

In the sky

On the seas

In the grave

Howling a cry

Singing a cry

Sobbing a cry

Who is crying

Someone living

Someone dying

Suckle the Sun

There is a yearning in all of us
That wockles toward the sun -
A blessed cre-ont so full of Zeus
With hope for joys to run.

Each with his mouse that nibs the straw,
Each his own tissle to brave.
I is a word like a bat in a cave
With wish for a bear to become.

Who hollows the pip from mouth to mouth?
Who is it who forms the kevaul?
It mutters the tongue through coyotes' night calls,
Through willows and winds and walls.

Each straw in the beak of Spring to begin
Is what I know to believe -
Is joy in a drop or mirth in despair -
Is wing on the breeze of desire.

Each man at dawn can suckle the sun
And tuckle a smile on his knee.

Learning to Walk

1. *A Child*

Balance first,
stabilize on two legs, standing
with walking to do. Put one leg
forward, then the other's turn,
no falling. Great. Now the next,
a hand on whatever's nearby.
I can do it. I can walk.

2. *An Old Man*

Balance first,
stabilize on two legs, standing
with walking to do. Put one leg
forward, then the other's turn,
no falling. Great. Now the next,
a hand on whatever's nearby.
I can do it. I can walk.

The Murky Spillway of My Pond
of Emotions

Water and light, glimpses
of liquid fish with proud stripes
of gold and white, eddies not knowing
which way to turn in the drenching
of this world.
                    We're walking a path
through cedars, an upward sloping stretch
cleared of everything except the gathering
of trees, the thick splotching of shadow and light,
a sense that something high-up has come down
as though some fancy cloud
decided to sleep at our feet
on a day showing more blue-green light
than any ever before –
when there could not be more
but there is.

The Abundance of Blue Out There

Even my imagination can't handle it.
Blue is so blue, so unique, so forever.
It does not stop inside the mind.

I'll try to build more imaginations
over those hills, down that long road,
with teams of engineers.

Maybe with an arcade of imaginations
there could be room enough:
never has so much held so much.

Bookstore

Geography books are the best. It's like going
down to Avenue K just to see what it's like, surprised
to see a tiger there.

History is dead and about the dead.
Until you realize you're reading
about us. Can you believe it?

Philosophy you can take or leave.
It would take you deep
but you won't understand it anyway.

Literature? It tries to persuade you to believe.

Religion? The most important of all, but a loser.
Believers and not, everything in between.
And wars.

Cooking. Puzzles. Crafts. Who's got the time?

And who'd read about mathematics?
Just let the books lie around.
As though you'd read them.

And physics. E equals m c squared. So what?
They think they know what's going on.
All that's out there. Can't shake
that it's got the only proof method in town.

Poetry? Well, well, well. Very bothersome.

ACGT

DNA. Which letter has the greatest supply,
and why? Does the answer tell me why I'm me,
and not a dog, or its flea?

De oxy ribo nu cleic a cid

Which letter is assigned to recall that word?

If I fling all of the letters into
the Okefenokee swamp
will they blossom forth
all the life that's ever frothed?

I look at those 4 letters
that make a double helix
and think what they do.

L I F E

I n f i n i t e l i f e.

Now I know my A C G T's.
Tell me what you think of me.

Why Go?

O minney moe miney
Might flu the ruke –
Not terra not luna but una:
O round such time as ends and overs,
O cross the null aleaping,
O thru the zoom aflume from ever
Where end and 'gin twincircle so sadly.

Why go moe so miney to any?
Lux and larn oercome the stickers;
And vision as misty as monsoons weeping
Soon creeping to coffin is kinder.
All morn's asun and dark's atwinkle
And green's so furious it dies a'being . . .
Why go moe when staying's so sticking?

Never have you seen such always nothing . . .
Great suns are quenched by simply not being.
Go on 'round where Lucifer faltered,
Breeze past God's old nursery nook:
End is so lost and time's no longer . . .
Go on moe and miney be with you.

Time's Nose

A stone-blind dog went ahowling to the heavens
Her pups sucked tears from snaggle-tooth weeds
She staggered through hedges of untrimmed years
Time was let loose to scavenge the waste.

Down out of herself came a scurry of curs
Births after births in a thick sick race
The mother-dog was the prey of prowling time
Herself the birth the breed and the death.

Thorn-sharp whistles are piercing her puppies
Their four-legged whimpering dry to the bone
She whines their cause to the tail-tucked seasons
But time has a nose for life's hot scent.

Losing My Younger Self

There are two of me
as I move into my 10th decade.

One of me is dragging the other along
into the decrepit zone,

that hard-wired me
throwing a ball, riding a horse,
making love, making my legs run.

My body clings to my younger self
while the me I am now begins to know

decrepitude when I rise from a chair,
when I try to walk a mile,
and if mounting a horse, I would fail.

We are trying to live together
but only one will prevail.

Floyd

Like the ghost that you are
you walk next to me, silent,
died last night, I feel
you breathing on me,
but softly, with love,
following me as we step.

I open the door and go through
noting where you are, close to me.

Yesterday we were talking to each other.
Living yesterday, and today, what?
If I stop to hug you, you disappear. I
speak words for you
to the air. Your lips do not move.

How long will we stay together,
my dear dead brother.

How High the Sky

Stave away, stave away,
Stave away death.
Run and row, pump some iron.
Work hard to delay my death.

But the day will come no matter
When I'll breathe that final breath.
How many walks will suffice?

But I am putting it off a while,
Keeping more time to breathe,
To sop my brain in the minutes left,
To gaze at the sky and say hi.

Say So

oh oh
what is so
body aches
that's its way

tell my soul
listen no
does not hear
or behold

something's there
flesh and hair
tiny wisps
in the air

see now child
far to go
life does laps
till go no

when dead
what's been said
pile of ashes
tiny flashes

wind comes blow
I feel gone
wind comes blow
I am gone

How Long, O Lord

The whipping tides of life
batter my brain. The weary-worn

cliffs, the scraggy scars,
the endless flow of sand.

This is my brain. This is its shore.

Puppets and Strings

This one is a philosopher
with few strings attached,
left to struggle alone, a leg akimbo,
an arm stretched out too far,
a head too large.

Next to the philosopher is a poet,
loose and wobbly, head in the sky
craning upward, water
wetting its wide-open eyes.

Next the painter, next the sculptor
or musician. A dancer with too many strings,
mesmerized by liquid sways and swoops,
whose limbs can't stop moving
until it collapses in a pile.

Most of the puppets behave just right,
all with plenty of strings,
rhythmic steps and leaps, all the same –
except the few alone who keep breaking
their strings.

The Jailkeeper

If you see me dangling
at the end of a rope
it's okay for you to ask

is he dancing or dying

Drop by Drop

As I
bend over
the wash basin
brushing
my teeth
each minute
drips away
alone
irretrievably
a faucet
I cannot
turn off

The End of Emptiness

An empty cardboard box is placed
in a fireplace fire.

It starts with small licks of flames
that leap big then faster big,

a fury that finds existence
from plants to trees to sawmill teeth,

cutting, chewing, squeezing, molding
a box, strong enough for holding.

But now its place and fate
are the goodbye swallows of this fire.

The jaws of flames.

As fast as fire.

Black is Blacker

I am inside a black hole.
No, I am the hole,

the maw where the present disappears.
The hole I am is all of my past.

When the hole is finished
I am nothing.

And the biggest black hole:
all the past that ever was

furiously trying to be
finished.

The Physician

My weakening knees
are the most telling,
then my hips, my aching feet,
the quickening of breaths.

I have foreseen this crumbling.

I read a columnist lament
that it's happening to her at only 61,
whereas I'm 91 so I weigh
the gift of 30 years.

But it's small help when I see omens
of the approaching end, when that dread word
will come.

But even I, a physician,
have no Christ-like Lazarus power.

Dots and Dashes

I'm not Beethoven nor am I
Michelangelo. Not Einstein nor Tolstoy.
The more giants named who have burned away
the more I can see the smoke of their hope.

How did they feel when they knew their weight?
What views did they have of little planets,
big birds, romping children, breath-stopping
cemeteries, marriages, mountain tops?

Oh I have my burning too.
It's good to be even some pencil caricature
of whatever is emerging
when you connect my dots.

Seed Bursting

Inside my skull, an unbroken hull

that holds the seed
like all seeds
that seem to know,
that swell
to find the opening—

Life's decree, outward and onward,
smacking my back,
sends me irreversibly into this world.

Someday the Future

They say we exist in a fantasy bubble.
I like that. I can shake off reality.

I don't have to see the melting
iceberg, the burning forest, the biblical

flood. Let it be a fantasy.
Let my granddaughter

and her children-to-come be my fantasies.

Zeus Around Water

Zeus around water is shaking and spilling
Moon sucking a thumbpie after spaces so filling
Ran ditches on mars and scorched hungry at noon
Blew trillions of yeses like yelping tossed inward.

Jar-rooster is cackling a crowbooster of begging
Himp and hump and limp and dump
Follow the eyes rolling against planets colliding
Against planets and nanets and waces in spaces.

Limp and dump, oh hump and himp
Heard tra-las instead, rocklashed and timesplashed
Tongue the forks of dipdragons in deathhaunt
Whistle beliefs while strutting in secret.

Struts a stroll and cats are cold, eyes yellow
Like eternity burning sulfuric incense, and seeping
Through coals of nightbogged creepers, self-stalked
And dawn-hoped in the middark of eyelanterns.

Everrise, neverrose, come up stiffsolid from ghost-lying
Evedropped that borning was breathing like sirens
Soothsayers divining that meadows breed silence
But borning is kerneled in nightcracking somewhere.

Cracking like gullets of spooked lightning
Wheezing down cobbled planets of timefury
No rest in thought before the spilling of thunder
The bursting and splatter of all that stormed under.

Ah for a billion years to hum in leisure
And more, much more, to yawn a dawn,
With one cocked eye to spy a vision
And time to sigh at it all.

The Smallest Way to Say It

Beauty.
No, truth.
No, insight.
No, meaning.
No, sound.
No, celebrate.
No, life.

So, try this:

Beautytruthinsightmeaningsoundcelebratelife.

A poem is language with high intention
strewn with failures, but cannot stop.

Silence Can Mean

when no bird sings,
when no leaf falls,

or when a snowflake
touches down.

It opens existence.

No need to answer
or to blink your eye.

Foggy Crystal Ball

What will happen in this world
of great concern
after I slip into my grave?

I've seen so much: a great
depression, a 2nd world
war, black blotches of little
wars, clouds of atomic bombs, twin
towers collapsing, a pandemic, global
climate change, maybe the closing chapter.

Some who died a hundred years ago
would not have anticipated,
would have had no room to imagine
what catastrophes might come.
And did.

So now my legs dangle at the grave.
After more than 90 years it's fair
for me to wonder.

What's Next after Old Age?

You know
but you know
you don't know.

Ode to the First Read

I've read Ulysses,
The Divine Comedy, Paradise Lost,
The Odyssey.

85

But a finer point:
the first read is gone,

that durable pith that quickened
my life, making me more.

What I Heard

Writing about the tweeting
of an unseen bird
in a nearby tree
is not the same
as hearing the tweet

while glooming along the path
beside the creek
flowing without a murmur
on a warm February day,
the sun in the company
of oaks and cedars,
gray moss dripping
from limbs laying shadows
like iron webs
on the face of the earth,

from a little throat,
a moment –
a tuneful unspellable sound.

In my quiet world today
the tweeting of that lone bird
may not be what saved my life
but made my life worth saving.

Words Cannot Say

These words are nothing more than what they are. They do
what words do, but cannot reach what they long for –

the call from the beak of a baby bird

the cat's soft purr,

the whimper of a lonely dog,

the coyote crying to the distant above,

the trumpet of a bull elephant,

the longing announcement of a lion at night,

the perfected song of a whale,

the soprano reaching high C,

the whinny of a horse to the audience of air,

the hum of a mother's lullaby,

the bow that quivers the violin string,

the English horn exhaling its sigh,

the solo piano playing Fur Elise to me.

. . . and she said, why did you write that?
And maybe I do not know.

Our Load

All of everything that has frothed and fused
its blind ways through the ages
and morphed into what it has now become
after what has passed,
has trickled down the seams,
preserving just a hint of me,
molded from the blows and dents,
the breaths and aches
of my living, sucked asunder,
into the flood of all that's past,
into the places that touch
the shores of our present.

So I say, you and I contain a bit
of all that's ever been; we are the present,

carrying our load into tomorrow.

How Many Paths

never unfold
but might have, could have,
when destiny's axe
falls this way instead of that.

My wife's heart stopped.
Her doctors saved her. Three minutes
more would have changed
the script.

What would have happened to me?
Another wife, another child not born,
a whole career, another way of life
to unfold for sure, did not.

Vapor trails that did not start.
Deaths side-stepped,
pitfalls I never fell into.

How many faces have I not seen,
how many words not spoken,
how many birds not ever in the sky,
how many lives have I not lived.

To say nothing about what happened
when my mother and father never met.

It's Writ Somewhere

The screw will unscrew
The nail will pull out
The horse will collapse
And I will not breathe

Oh, throw away that book
So the temple will stand.

Time Passes without Mercy

La Belle Vie Sans Merci

As evidence I offer for your consideration
That Antarctica is the leftover piece of continental
Fragmentation and drift taking some time of course
Remaking earth its animals survival rules
Changing unannounced nothing to hint how done it is
Without asking any pardon the grind grinds on and on.

Did I say big bang, galaxies, star bursts, detritus
Pooling into planets our very own where we what words
Where we live and die while that something in between melts away.

Where we live and die in a heartbeat with nothing nothing
To take note of us before oblivion seeps in
What was that they will ask was it a planet.

More to the point of here and now my wrinkles
Wrinkle up my face have I looked in the mirror lately
My wife died everybody I know has died or will soon
And I am spooning my grave hole down to one last spoon
When I hope that mercy will give it all one
Just at that moment one
Catch this if you can one
Little wink.

A Person Comes In at Will

Even the dead ones,
especially the dead ones –

Oh, there she is, my Mother,
just as she used to be.
Oh, if she could only speak to me,
just as she used to.

How wonderful I can call her forth
at will. I swear to you, there she is.

I stand like Hamlet with empty hands.
If I work at it, I can hear her voice.

I am getting to that land
where I will join them near
the flowing river.

Unsayable

If Beethoven had not been born
If Beethoven had not composed it
We would not have that glory
We would not have his symphony nine

Nor the fifth nor all the rest
Of those miracles uncaped
Of what floods the region of souls
That dwell among the stars

In the universe's whole expanse
In all of space and span
His music burst the bubble of beauty
And that gift might not have been

Oh foolish words dare you say it
Say so feebly that unsayable thing

I Hope I Will Not Die

Even though it's a hopeless hope,
even though I am only a candle
burning to stay alive,
the burning itself my ending.

No matter that so much help is stacked around me:
doctors, hospitals, medications, ambulances.
No matter the spas, fitness trainers, exercise.

No matter the laughter, family,
friendships, jokes and games, floating
around the house of smiles.

No matter that my trail
was once a primrose path. No matter grieving
countless deaths.

Though I've had fervent hopes come true
you will be right to think of me
as a green candle snuffing out.

Talking with My Brother Frank

Frank, I can't talk with you now that you've died.

Bill, yes you can. We're talking now.
Hearing my voice out loud is not required.
In your head and in your heart I'm here with you
and always will be.
Whenever you want we'll talk just like we used to Skype.
We talked and talked and held our faces in our eyes.
We'd say let's talk and like magic we did.

But Frank, that's different. You were there
in your room, your head and hands.
Your voice, your own chosen words,
your ears that you used for hearing me,
to listen so well.

Bill, Bill. Listen to me now. Open yourself
to know the magic of life and death.
Yes, the magic, the power we have.
What is happening now, right now?
We are talking, you and I.
You are able to call me whenever you choose.
And I will call you, when you are sitting and sculpting,
I will come right in, while you are quiet and ready.
Is this not magic enough?
While you are gazing at the moon,
I will come right up to you,
and we will look into that night sky together.
You know this is true, Bill.
Just look at what is here for you and me.
Just look. It's here in us.
Aren't we lucky, Bill?
Yes, Frank. Absolutely, yes.

Somewhere the End

I came upon an old man he was crying
I asked is it because you're dying

This is what to me he told
No he said it's because I'm old

But the life you've lived I see was good
Had your choices did what you could

Sometimes good sometimes sad
Now I'm old my body's turned bad

But you see sunshine you hear rain
Your mind is sound your thoughts are sane

We are born, live, grow old, die
A mystery so quick never know why

Now see I why you cry.

Gasp Again

Tis a pity to lose that sudden gasp
That leaps out upon a sunrise
After too many it fades away
A slow effusion of miracles eroded

That first unveiling that stops the breath
Like volcanic bubbles that skyward rise
Which we see in that holy while
And feel our soul have its smile

We take our turns as we journey
Through this tumbleweed world
Along the cosmic stream of ups and downs
Of what rubs in and what rubs out

With hope it'll come to pass
As we watch the final end of day
A tear on our cheek of salty regret
When we gasp again at the blazing sunset

Dying Time Sonnet

The song that comes at death
we like to think
will be soft,
a sugar-bath.

We like to dreamily feel an end
without an end, wings lifting
quietly to some dwelling in the sky
where love abounds.

We cannot end, this we know.
Lullaby breathing, gentle thoughts
slipping slowly slowly away,
believing there is no end.

Death has no sting. Takes no notice
when darkness turns off.

All We Are

Among the stars we are gathered on our turning globe,
it comes to this, our lonely sitting stools:

Now all we are is running as water from our palms.
We clinch our useless fists to clutch ourselves.
We drain into the past that looms dark and dead.
We are caught in the guilt of life,
the space of past and dead, out beyond
the edge of all our star-sprinkled limits of vision
and further, as the voice of full-blown self
speaks relentlessly at the bitter blank of time and space.

Gather us then O holy murderous Time
that runs through our house and hearts
like smells of death astride a wind
feeling the openness of our doors:

Now, then, gather us like petals clinging to our flower
and tell us a passing word of beauty
and who we are
and what beyond the blazing sky we may hope to drown into
and whether if there be soul
will it fling itself aloft
like a bird loosened from gravity
or will it clutch the bones of our daily cares,
the only cares we have known
as dusting teapots on cloudy afternoons
or paying dues of three cents more than just,
and mothers sleeping in our milky bones
and fathers beating their heads against our coffin walls
and we the fumbling introduction they were striving for:

Or if the soul alas is a part of us
and falls at death in the same dark hole
and flees at death along the alleys
that whine endlessly across forever
or if when we die it is the soul that dies
or if in fact our bones come clean
and when the marrow is gone
there's no soul to be seen
and if in fact we are temporal things that strut and fake
and shout despair and sit and hold to a tearless pose

then let us rest, and take a pause, and loose our hands
and watch Time flow away from us.

If I Were Stuck in a Desert

and saw a dead leaf
it would give me joy

and a bug creeping along its life
I would feel the awe

spotting a bird in flight
I would cry

or just a cup of sand
pouring from my hand

and when I look at the midnight sky
would I believe my eyes

beauty and mystery
lift me high

Age Happens

As my age mounts on the scales of time
I want my fate to be like a child,
to see the simple stuff of life
with the freshness of a just-now rose.

The Spring re-occurs and re-occurs
year by year like daily dawns.
I love you, Life, like a kiss

that never grows old, that never dies,
a bottomless fresh-water joy,
the way a child in a carriage
gleams in the sunshine patch of beginning.

Your Beginning

As swishing a wand unveils the surprise of Spring,
the flourish of a flower's wild panache of colors,
the sky's brighter twinkle by just one new star,
or the warm sun breaking open for us a new day . . .

So the wand that opened the universe, that same wand
that cracks open all seeds and eggs,
has waived forth your birth, *voilá*, your beginning.

Lights! Lights! The thrill! The thrill of it!

Your beginning is today the second of April,
Two Thousand and Eight years after the counting began.
You are the first for your parents and grandparents.
You are called Edie Jane Guest. That's your name.

You, with your mother and father, may take a bow.

How we waited – your parents, grandparents, all!
But you waited too, bathing in primordial nectar.
It seemed long to us, holding our breath, like you.
How long did it seem to you, waiting to begin?

But even magic cannot ever uncape from nothing.
Yes, you will know that beginnings have histories –
the roil of the world, chancy links of lives and lives,
improbables turning like sleight-of-hand into inevitable – **to you.**

Your mother and father know that someday you will fleet
away from their arms, and still they will help to prepare you.

Please, dwell a while with them, with all of us.
Your new bath will be the nectar of love.

Today as you are born, your baby feet step
upon a stage of streaming cornucopic life, plying
light, shadow, green, blue, song, love, laugh, cry, dream, yearn –
this and more will be in your arms, my dear, like roses.

As your grandfather, writing with you in my mind,
I feel my heart beating,
when I think of you at your beginning.

Go, now, Edie Jane, it is your time to begin.

About Atmosphere Press

Founded in 2015, Atmosphere Press was built on the principles of Honesty, Transparency, Professionalism, Kindness, and Making Your Book Awesome. As an ethical and author-friendly hybrid press, we stay true to that founding mission today.

If you're a reader, enter our giveaway for a free book here:

SCAN TO ENTER
BOOK GIVEAWAY

If you're a writer, submit your manuscript for consideration here:

SCAN TO SUBMIT
MANUSCRIPT

And always feel free to visit Atmosphere Press and our authors online at atmospherepress.com. See you there soon!

www.ingramcontent.com/pod-product-compliance
Lightning Source LLC
Chambersburg PA
CBHW020734160726
47993CB00006B/2440